SERIES EDITOR: RANI T.

Student + Teacher		Teacher-only	
a animations	**ia** activities	**lp** lesson plans	**tn** teacher's notes
ilt instructor-led tutorials	**w** worksheets	**w** worksheets	**ak** answer keys
g games	**v** videos		
audio			

Preface

Collins Little Learners, comprising 20 books in all, provides graded, age-appropriate learning opportunities targeting holistic skill development for children in the age group of 3 years to 6 years. Spread across three levels, the series spans **English**, **Maths**, **General Awareness**, **Art and Craft** and **Hindi**. The series comes bundled with a **workbook** for English and a book of **rhymes and stories** for each level. The books use a combination of hands-on activities, frequent recapitulation and child-friendly artwork to facilitate learning.

The early years are the most significant years for growth, development and learning. During this period, children need adequate opportunities for stimulating experiences as these favourably affect various learning abilities. Learning experiences, when chosen and planned properly, fuel the innate curiosity of children, and stimulate their thought processes.

Learning and Development During the Early Years

The goal of learning during the early years is to enhance the all-round development of personality and to inculcate healthy attitudes, life skills and good values. Creative play, well thought-out games and developmentally appropriate activities help children develop the necessary skills to achieve these goals. The skills that children need to acquire can broadly be categorized as:

Motor: Motor skills pertain not only to gross motor activities like walking and jumping but also include fine motor activities like the ability to hold a pencil and write. The development of motor skills is facilitated through several graded activities.

Personal, Social and Emotional: Personal, social and emotional development, necessary for the overall personality development of children, is achieved using a combination of hands-on activities, role plays and thought-provoking stories and rhymes.

Linguistic: The ability to listen, speak, read and write is critical to success in formal learning environments.

Mathematical: The development of mathematical ideas and concepts is important at this stage since children will continue to build on this learning for most of their years of schooling.

Knowledge and Understanding of the World: This is achieved through activities that enable children to explore their surroundings at home and in the school, and interact with the people that they see around them.

Health and Safety: The idea of health and safety is introduced through activities, stories and retelling of real-life experiences to encourage children to focus on health and well-being.

Creative: Creative skills are developed through a host of activities involving art, craft, painting, roleplays, etc.

Logical and Rational Thinking: Activities that involve simple puzzles, pattern-completion and visual discrimination help children develop logical and rational thinking skills.

The Collins Little Learners Teacher Support Materials

The series includes extensive teacher support in the form of:

Teacher's Resource Books: Comprises stories, activity banks, classroom management and assessment guidelines

Multimedia eBook: Consists of animations, audio, video, slide shows and interactive exercises

Print-ready Worksheets: Additional worksheets for practice and reinforcement, present in the digital support

Digital Flashcards: Flashcards with embedded sounds and animations for letter formation and letter-sound association

Animations and Songs: Animated stories and rhymes set to tune

Interactive Games: Interactivities to reinforce concepts in a fun and engaging manner

A note on the activity banks (included in the Teacher's Manuals)

The activity banks comprise hands-on activities that will help children develop the requisite skills to attain age-appropriate learning goals. In keeping with Howard Gardener's theory of multiple intelligences, the activity banks include options and variations that enable teachers to provide a planned cycle of experiences and opportunities, which foster each type of intelligence, to every child in their classrooms. The activity banks equip teachers to use the strengths of children as a means of complementing their less developed areas by valuing and nurturing the inherent abilities of the children.

Contents

I Can Write A–D

Write the letters A–D.

A A

B B

C C

D D

I Can Write E–H

Write the letters E–H.

E  E

F  F

 G G

H  H

I Can Write I–L

Write the letters I–L.

I Can Write M–P

Write the letters M–P.

M M  N N 

 O O P  P

I Can Write Q–T

Write the letters Q–T.

Q Q R R

S S T T

I Can Write U–X

Write the letters U–X.

U U  V V 

W  W X  X

I Can Write Y–Z

Write the letters Y–Z.

Join the dots to complete the picture. Colour it.

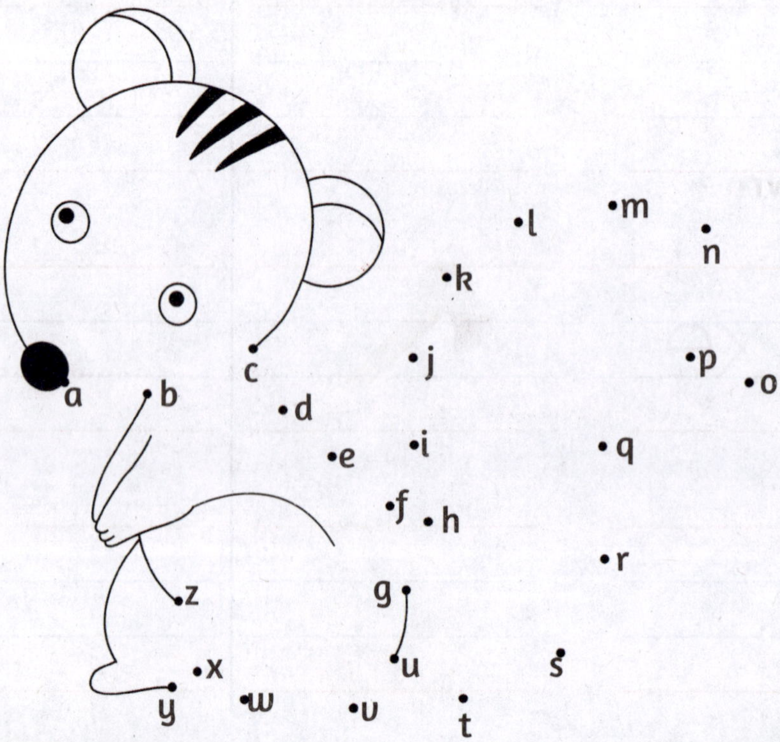

Hello Letter Aa

Trace and write a.

a a a a a

Write the missing letter.

......xe 

......nt 

......pple 

......nkle 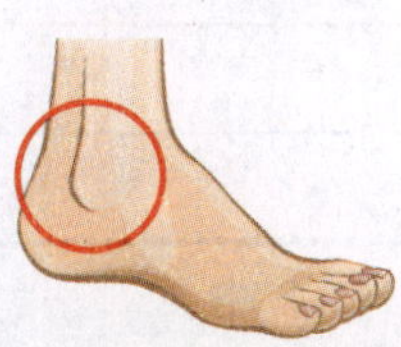

Hello Letter Bb

Trace and write b.

b b b b b

Write the missing letter.

.... ox 

.... in 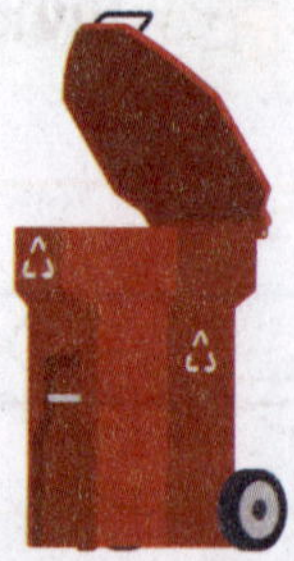

.... oy 

.... ed 

Hello Letter Cc

Trace and write c.

c c c c c

Write the missing letter.

.......up 

.......at 

.......ot 

.......an 

Hello Letter Dd

Trace and write d.

d d d d d

Write the missing letter.

....a 

....ig 

....en 

....ot 

I Know!

Look at the pictures. Name them. Write a/an before them. One has been done for you.

an 

Choose the correct word.

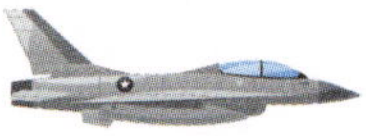

this that

this that

this that

this that

Hello Letter Ee

Trace and write e.

e e e e e

Write the missing letter.

_ gg 

_ ngin _ 

_ lbow 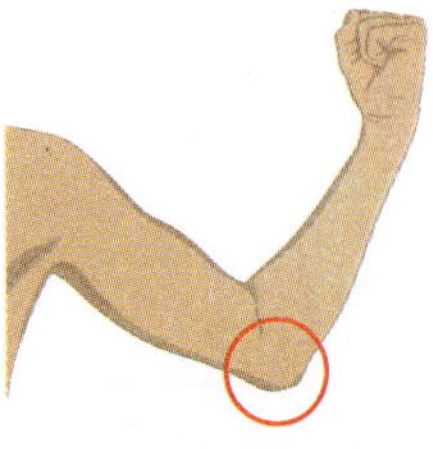

_ l _ phant 

Hello Letter Ff

Trace and write f.

f f f f f

Write the missing letter.

.... at 

.... ig 

.... un 

.... an 

Hello Letter Gg

Trace and write g.

g g g g g

Write the missing letter.

.... um 

.... oat 

.... irl 

.... rass 

Hello Letter Hh

Trace and write h.

h h h h h

Write the missing letter.

.............at 

.............ut 

.............ug 

.............en 

I Know!

Circle the correct word.

bat

bats

hat

hats

ball

balls

apple

apples

bear

bears

cup

cups

Choose the correct word.

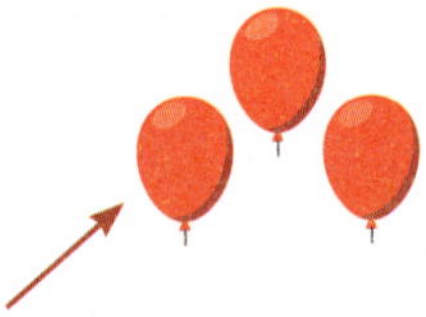

these those

these those

these those

these those

Hello Letter Ii

Trace and write i.

i i i i i

Write the missing letter.

......gloo

Ind......a

......nk

f......n

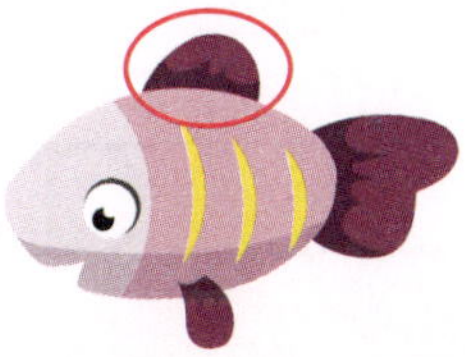

Hello Letter Jj

Trace and write j.

j j j j j

Write the missing letter.

........ump  ....ar 

........am  ....og 

Hello Letter Kk

Trace and write k.

k k k k k

Write the missing letter.

.... ing

.... ite

.... ettle

.... itten

Hello Letter Ll

Trace and write l.

Write the missing letter.

.... ad 

.... eg 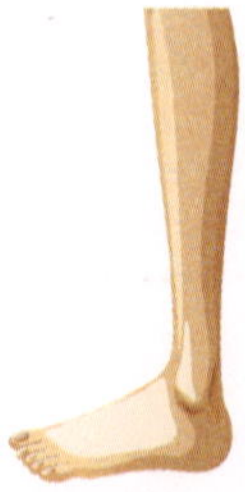

.... og 

.... ip 

I Know!

Match the picture to the correct group of words.

egg beside a pan

cat inside the box

hen under a tree

cup between jars

rat on a mat

Hello Letter Mm

Trace and write m.

m m m m m

Write the missing letter.

.... ug

.... an

.... o ....

.... at

Hello Letter Nn

Trace and write n.

n n n n n

Write the missing letter.

____et 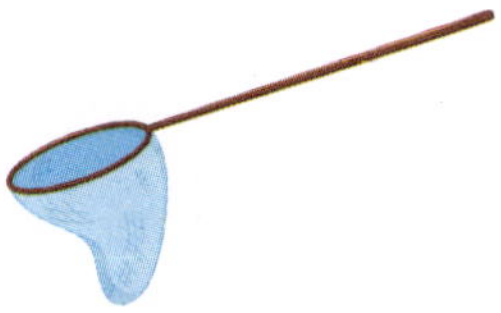

____est 

____ib 

____i____e 

Hello Letter Oo

Trace and write o.

Write the missing letter.

........range 

........strich 

........tter 

........x 

I Know!

Match the picture to the correct word.

	sing
	sleep
	run
	jump
	read

Hello Letter Pp

Trace and write p.

p p p p p

Write the missing letter.

......ot 

......en 

......u...... 

......eg 

Hello Letter Qq

Trace and write q.

q q q q q

Write the missing letter.

.............uilt 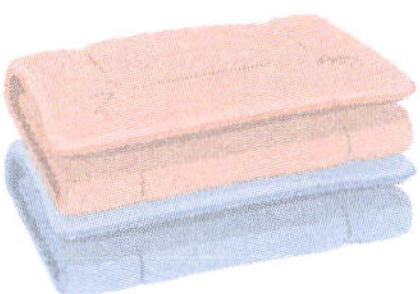 ....uail 

.............uiet  ....ueen 

Hello Letter Rr

Trace and write r.

r r r r r

Write the missing letter.

..........at 

..........od 

..........ug 

..........un 

Hello Letter Ss

Trace and write s.

s s s s s

Write the missing letter.

......it

......un

......oap

......ip

Hello Letter Tt

Trace and write t.

t t t t t

Write the missing letter.

......op 

......ag 

......en 10

......in 

I Know!

Look at the pictures. Write the correct word. One has been done for you.

I he she we they

I

Hello Letter Uu

Trace and write u.

u u u u u

Write the missing letter.

.............rn 

.............p 

.............mpire 

.............nder 

Hello Letter Vv

Trace and write v.

v v v v v

Write the missing letter.

........et 

......ulture 

........an 

........ase 

Hello Letter Ww

Trace and write w.

w w w w w

Write the missing letter.

......et 

......ag 

......ed 

......ash 

Hello Letter Xx

Trace and write x.

x x x x x

Write the missing letter.

fo..........

bo..........

..........-mas

..........-ray

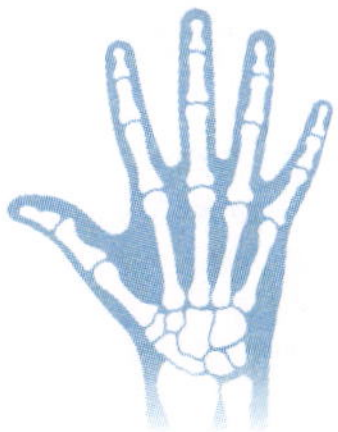

Sight Words!

Read the sight words. Write them in the correct place on the wall.

I

is I up get mother away father

am brown are uncle happy

Hello Letter Yy

Trace and write y.

y y y y y

Write the missing letter.

..........ak

..........acht

..........oga

..........ellow

Hello Letter Zz

Trace and write z.

z z z z z

Write the missing letter.

....ebra 

....ero 

....ig-....ag 

....ip 

I Know!

Circle the correct question word.

what | who

who | what

who | where

who | where

who | where

who | where

I Know Letter Sounds!

Look at the pictures. Name them. Write the first letter.

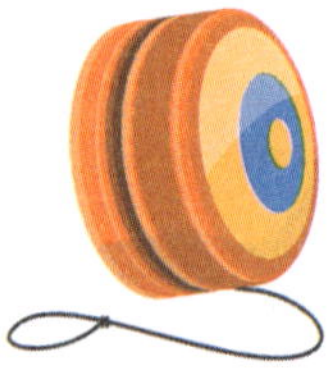

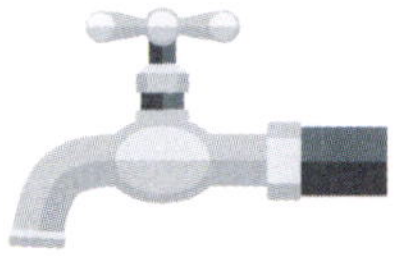

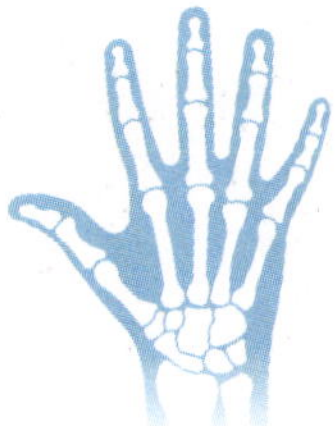

I Can Write Letters!

Write the missing capital and small letters.

Aa

C

d

E

G

h

I

k

l

N

p

q

S

U

w

X

Z

I Can Write Letters!

Write the missing capital and small letters.

Aa

F

K

P

U

Y

Teacher's Note: If the children are ready, this can be made challenging by making it a time-bound activity.

I Can Write Words!

Using the help box, write the names of the pictures.

lad tin man nib van bin rat sad cap

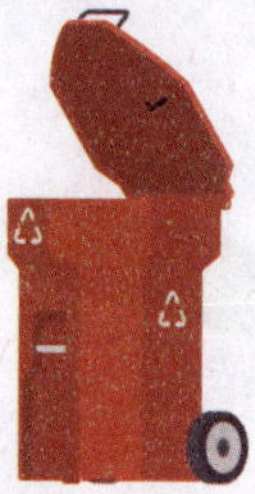

I Can Write Words!

Using the help box, write the names of the pictures.

jet dog vet peg den hen top cot pod

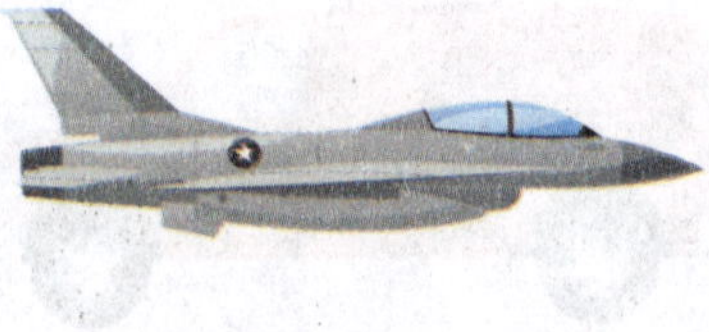

I Can Write Words!

Using the help box, write the names of the pictures.

bat sun dot rug bed sun box sit bun

I Can Read Secret Words!

Write the beginning letter of each word. Write the new word!

I Can Read Secret Words!

Write the beginning letter of each word. Write the new word!

Rhyme Along!

Write rhyming words for the words below. Use the help box. One has been done for you.

bin dig pen mat vet rat

cat — mat

hat —

hen —

tin —

wet —

fig —

Rhyme Along!

Write rhyming words for the words below. Use the help box. One has been done for you.

bag bed den lid sun van

men	bun	tag
den		

pan	wed	kid

I Can Write!

Look at the pictures. Write the missing letters.

ay ai

tr__ __n

pl__ __

s__ __l

m__ __l

p__ __nt

d__ __

s__ __

pr__ __

I Can Write!

Look at the pictures. Write the missing letters.

e ee ea ie y i

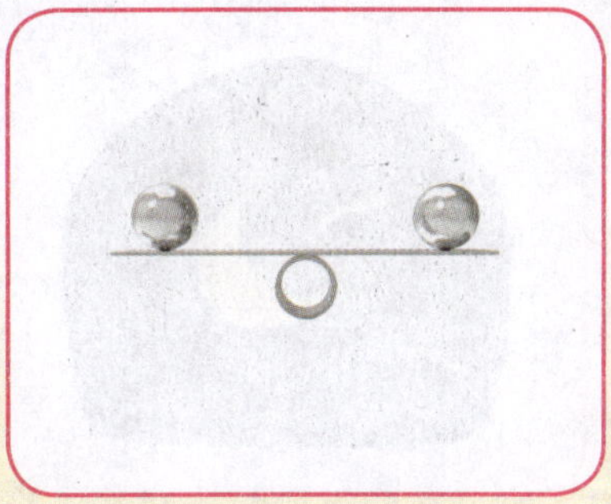

__qual

r__ __d

b__ __

f__ __ld

t__dy

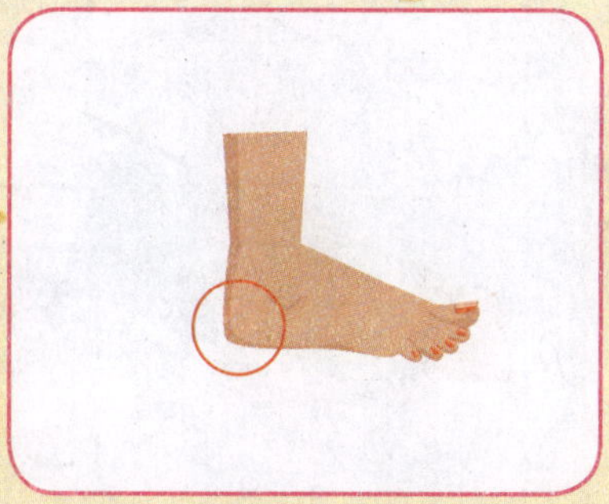

h__ __l

l__ __f

__ __t

I Can Write!

Look at the pictures. Write the missing letters.

ie y i

__ron

__ce

n__ght

dr__

t__ __

__ce cream

b__te

fl__

I Can Write!

Look at the pictures. Write the missing letters.

o   oa   oo   oe   ow

r__ __m

n__

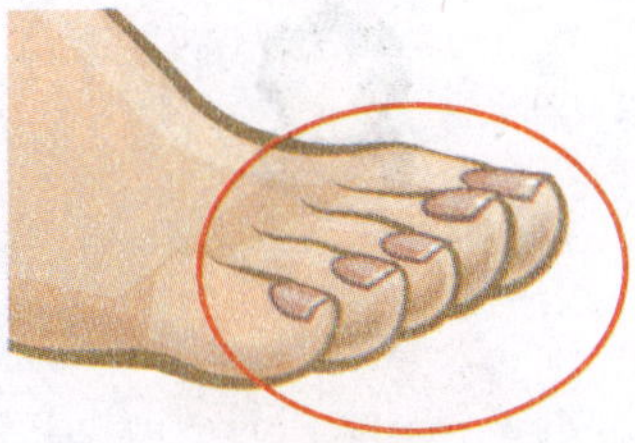

t__ __s

g__ __t

sl__ __

p__ __l

s__ __p

c__ __t

I Can Write!

Look at the pictures. Write the missing letters.

u ew ue a

n__ __

__tensil

gl__ __

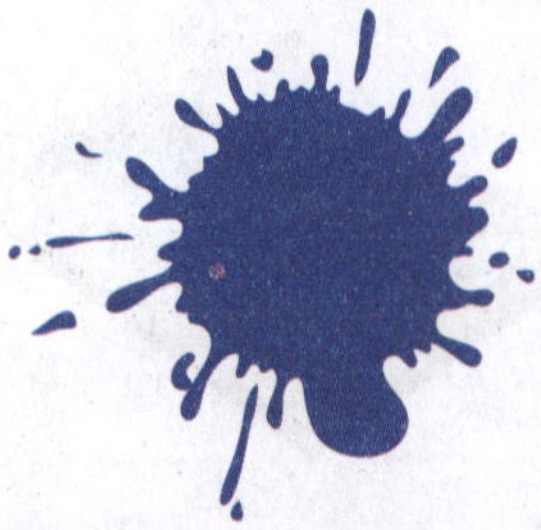

bl__ __

__niform

c__ke

t__be

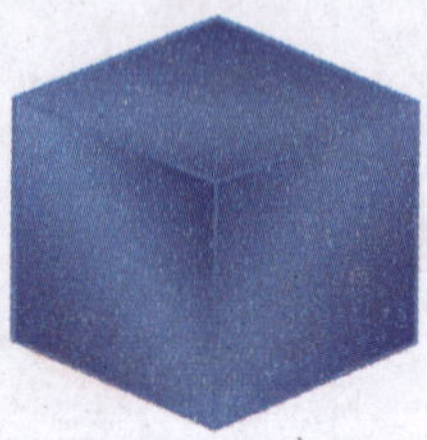

c__be

I Know!

Fill in the missing letters. Use the help box.

a ai ea oo ew i oa ow

__ron

l__ __f

f__ __

r__ __d

gr__ __

r__ __m

__ce

tr__ __n

I Can Read Secret Words!

Write the beginning letter of each word. Write the new word!

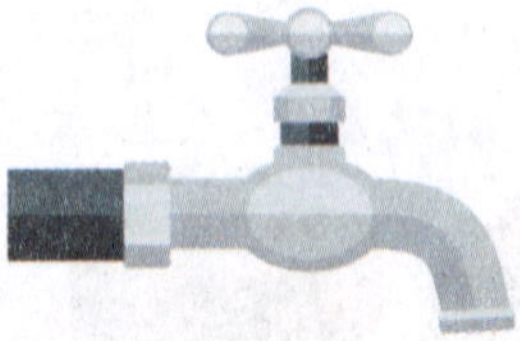

I Can Read Secret Words!

Write the beginning letter of each word. Write the new word!

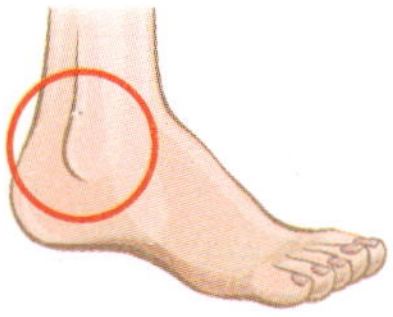

I Can Write!

Look at the pictures. Write the missing letters.

wh sh th ch

__ __ip

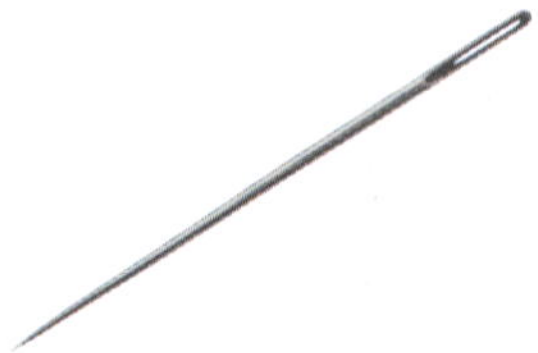

__ __in

__ __air

__ __ale

__ __irp

__ __ree

__ __ell

__ __isk

I Can Write!

Look at the pictures. Write the missing letters.

wh sh th ch

__ __elf

__ __ips

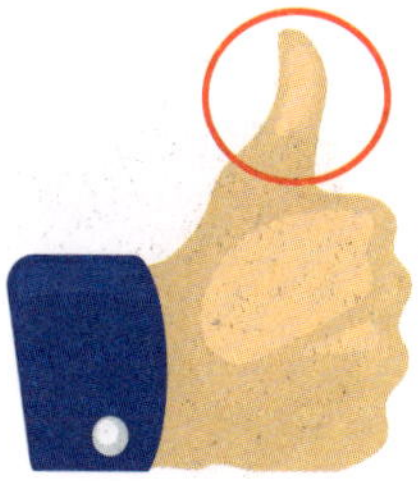

__ __umb

__ __ite

__ __ain

__ __eel

__ __is

__ __ere

I Can Write!

Fill in the missing letters. Use the help box.

sp bl sm cr gr pl st dr

__ __ack

__ __ant

__ __um

__ __ass

__ __ow

__ __ile

__ __in

__ __ar

I Can Write!

Fill in the missing letters. Use the help box.

gl sn fl sp br st cl sn

__ __oor

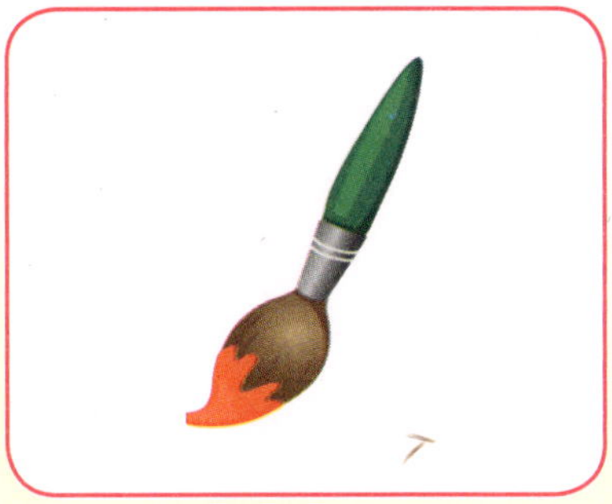

__ __ush

__ __ock

__ __ass

__ __own

__ __ake

__ __ill

__ __op

I Can Write!

Look at the pictures. Write the missing letters.

nk nd ng sk

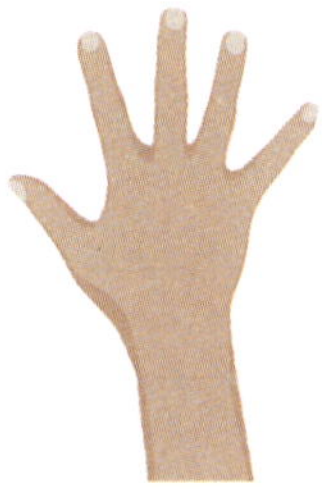

ha__ __

pi__ __

ri__ __

ma__ __

si__ __

de__ __

si__ __

sa__ __

I Can Read Secret Words!

Write the beginning letter of each word. Write the new word!

 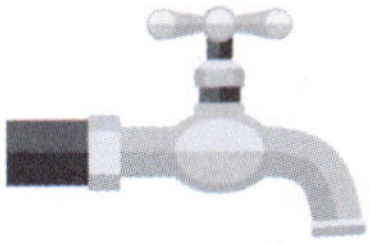  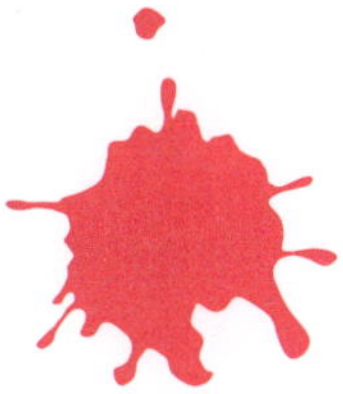

I Can Write!

Look at the pictures. Write the missing letters.

rr ss ll tt

ta__ __

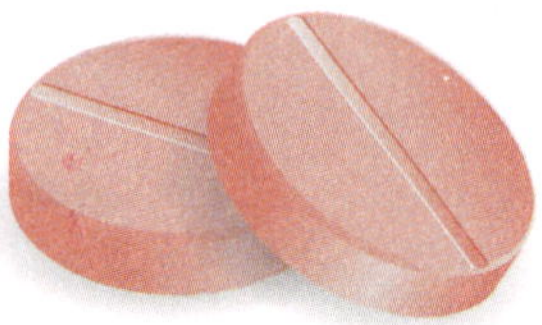

pi__ __

ro__ __

gra__ __

che__ __y

je__ __y

he__ __o

ki__ __en

I Can Write!

Look at the pictures. Write the missing letters.

rr ss ll tt

ba__ __

ye__ __ow

bu__ __

ki__ __

strawbe_ _y

lo__ __ipop

so__ __y

bu__ __er

Rhyme Along!

Write rhyming words for the words below. Use the help box. One has been done for you.

fly ball kiss shiny tea say

day	tiny	sea	hiss	cry	tall
say					

Rhyme Along!

Write rhyming words for the words below. Use the help box. One has been done for you.

grow clean bill blue ring coat

glue — blue

ill —

boat —

slow —

king —

bean —

Jumbled Words!

Look at the pictures. Write the correct spellings.

ngere

ihrst

ncrae

iksn

hirpc

sehos

Jumbled Words!

Look at the pictures. Write the correct spellings.

acke

aops

ante

ktie

lble

abder

I Can Write Sentences!

Look at the pictures. Write the correct group of words.

a small ant	a tall tree	an empty jug
a black dog	a big mango	a red box

I Can Write Sentences!

Make sentences using the group of words from the previous page. Remember to put a full stop at the end of each sentence! One has been done for your.

This is a big mango.

I Can Write Sentences!

Look at the picture. Complete the sentences. Use the help box.

is reading   is walking   is sitting   is playing